Homelands

For my mother IYA EFETI.

Under the Motando mo Wuwa – where chickens sleep at night – in your kitchen, Mama,
I first learned beauty in the word 'Zrizra' – when sleep consumes a child, yet they fight, short burst of five seconds power naps, shaking as one wakes, feeling as if one were about to fall off a cliff.
Under the Motando mo Wuwa in your kitchen,
I saw a baby chick standing on its mother's back, 'zrizraying'.

Homelands

Eric Ngalle Charles

Seren is the book imprint of
Poetry Wales Press Ltd.
Suite 6, 4 Derwen Road, Bridgend, Wales, CF31 1LH
www.serenbooks.com
facebook.com/SerenBooks
twitter@SerenBooks

ISBN: 9781781726549
Ebook: 9781781726556

A CIP record for this title is available from the British Library.

The publisher acknowledges the financial assistance of the Books Council of Wales.

Cover artwork: 'young ruler / cultural heritage' by Gobina Boris Nganje. Oil on canvas,
60 × 60 cm.

Printed in Bembo by Severn, Gloucester.

Contents

Cameroon

Tandami/Ngelleh

When *Tandami* and *Ngelleh* held
hands, running,
a little dog laughed.

When *Nyaka Mbusra* was whipped to death,
she jumped over the moon,
a little dog laughed.

When *Enjema* was seen kissing *Limunga*,
a little dog laughed,
barking mad,
all the way to the high priest.
(Kissing is frowned upon.)

Holding hands, running,
Tandami and *Ngelleh* laughed.
The little dog disappeared.
Nyaka Mbusra jumped over the moon.

Tandemi: Dish
Ngelleh: Spoon
Nyaka Mbusra: Last Cow

Child's Eyes

We grew up in uncertainty,
living in anticipation
of the unknown.
This did not stop us from living.

For so long we wondered what
may or may not come from
behind the city walls.

For now, we will make
airplanes with mango leaves,
untangle barbwires, slowly, to
make car parts.

We shall mash-up hibiscus plants,
lubricants for our car wheels,
as we wonder, what may
or may not come from
behind these city walls.

We hide
under an Iroko tree
sheltering us
from that harsh sun,
the future.

Iya: mother of many children

She carried you on her lap singing
lamentations of *'Njilanyame'* until
the houses that starved
were fed.
Serenading your ears with
'Izruki'
'Immukka'.
Recounting to you names
of those who left:
Ngomba
Mondowa
Njie
Libika

Sing to her,
Iya sing.
So,
she may follow your voice to
the entrance of Gbea, meet
her brothers,
kiss her sisters
Enanga
Eposi
Ndolo
Ndinge
Enjema
Clara
Iya,
carry her on your lap,
wings on which she drifts, until
the Gods in conjunction chant

Mezringwane
Mezrazringwane
Mezringwane

Njilanyame: Lion
Mezringwane: clean
Mezrazringwane: unclean
Mezringwane: clean
This is a spiritual incantation, inviting the spirits of the dead to come and make merry with the living. It always ends with *Mezringwane*.
Ending the incantation with *Mezrazringwane* means leaving open a portal for unclean spirits.

Kitchen

In my mother's kitchen, as
a boy before my mother
could sing:
        'Njinja-Aa-Ma-Temeh.'
Even before I was three months
old, I ate *Matambu*, food my
mother chewed before putting
in my mouth.

'Njinja-Aa-Ma-Temeh': Our mothers would sing this song, encouraging us to walk
towards them, they would entice us with food.

Tea Pluckers

Our mothers,
we do not remember the throes
of our sheroes, no one
remembers their names
until they die.

Mami Constance, gone
Mami Lucas, gone
Mami Ngwa, gone
Mami Josephine 'returned to the forest yesterday'

Baskets on shoulders, holes on
forehead, gaps, carvings, each
furrow hollow, deep, holding
pools of sweat dropping on their
tongues. They do not look right
nor left, heads down,
talking in tiny whispers, hands
picking young buds, fresh tea
leaves, trudging, no one
remembers their names until
payday.

Mami Joe, can I?
Mami Rita can I?
Mami Njie can I?
Juvenile
demands.

When it rains,
they pluck,
when sun comes,
they pluck
from early dawn
to dusk,
for pittance,
our mothers.

As for Iya Efeti,
my mother sits on loading bays waiting,
for when the women would come,
weighing their loads,
a brief rest for their backs.

"You only weigh na three kilos today?"

"Weh ma 'ami ngalle, you know say after we be finish work,
I be go help Ebong ei ma 'ami for plant yam for Kumba road Farm.
'Na we pikin them go kill we."

"Nooo ma 'ami, na guvment go kill we."

Soothsayer

We came,
Soothsayer invoked her father's ghost,
and summoned other spirits:

Ekulekule
Jukuke,
Nyango Na Mwanna
Evasra Mote
Mokele Mbembe

We assembled at night, in a children's graveyard,
when clock tick-toc-toed to midnight.

"Tonight, the village is calm," she intones,
pulling her audience into the spirit world,
her tongue casting spells, words swooping like bats.

She sits on a gravestone, haggard, clothed in rags,
she brings forth ghosts armed with razor blades
with blood dripping, glaring. She brings forth
night crawlers, dancing ants and maggots.

Her listeners, crossing borders under dark skies,
slept, shying from hard homeland fortunes.

Again, she appeared, Soothsayer,
channeling her father's ghost: his face with its open mouth,
dripping blood. In the glow she danced and paused and danced
again, then called her father's name, out loud, five times.

Elinge
Elinge
Elinge
Elinge
Elinge ....

Ekulekule: Tortoise, the wise one in Bakweri folklore.

Jukuke: A spirit of ill repute.

Nyango Na Mwanna: A goddess, also know as Mami Water. She resides in the Atlantic Ocean.

Evasra Mote: A half-stone and half-human god, he is the guardian of Mount Hvako (Mount Cameroon).

Mokele Mbembe: He roams the Congo Basin. He warned the Congolese people of the fate of Patrice Lumumba. They ignored his warnings. On the 17th of January 1961, at the age of 35, Patrice Lumumba was assassinated, becoming a martyr for the wider pan-African movement.

Elinge: A spiritual light.

Emolana

At night, the songs of an Izru woke me.
I followed its voice deep into the Kortoh of Wovilla village,
next to my grandfather's grave.
We met, you'd imprison summer in your smiles,
flowering, you leaned forward, whispering, shivering.
I returned home.
Sitting under the *Motando mo* Wuwa
in my mother's kitchen,
I wrote my vows on the walls.
Mba noo lingani Zrai Zrai.

Emolana: Beautiful lady
Izru: Owl
Mba noo lingani Zrai Zrai: I like you very much

Conception

Behind the krall we met,
one night and that was all,
a tiny drop of wine,
her hands on my spine,
little breeze whispering behind our ears,
stiffened buttocks up and down, we
rode on pacing steed, again and again.
On that cold night
behind the kraal and
out-of-sight, my
dear child, that
night you were
conceived.

Small Black Box

Under my mother's bed
is a small black box,
bruised – a small hole on
one side through which
as a child I saw the
world, bending.

Box filled with pencils of different colours:
brown, blue, yellow, red, indigo purple, green,
pink, teal, orange, light blue, pink, light green,
magenta, sky blue grey, lime green, violet
turquoise, aqua, beige, royal blue, sea green,
indigo, lilac, periwinkle …

In my dreams, I have opened this box many times,
painting pictures of my mother, carrying a brown
basket, plucking tea leaves from a plantation.
I coloured her in green as she cooked, aqua as she
watered the plants, light green as she planted,
dark green as she harvested, lilac as she invited
the chickens to their narrow perch.

I painted my mother wearing a sea green
sweater, navy blue scarf, lavender head tie,
cyan shoes. She once carried a tan handbag,
dangling, just by her waistline as she walked
me to school.

Many years later
when I was thirty-
seven and my mother
seventy-two, I took
solace, knowing she
would not smack me
as she used to when I
was a boy, when I was
plagued by stubbornness,

or call me Eric when I
angered her.

I asked my mother:

"Mama, the black box under your bed,
the bruised one, with a small hole on its side,
filled with pencils of all colours,
can I open it?"

My mother, as if expecting my
question, disappeared into her room.
There it was, a black box, she blew,
dusted it with her handkerchief. She
opened the box, she handed me a
picture. That was the first time I met
my father, after thirty-seven years in
a black box under her bed, my mother
was hiding my father.

If Heaven Is Her Father's Land, Her Father Can Keep It

For my sister, Queenta

Let the rains come in June not August.

Yes,
She wants to go where *Evasrikuke* sings:
where she can grow *Mbasri* side by side,
where *Eznuli* sucks nectar with bees as companions,
where water flows from *Hvako* through rocks
feeding the grass fields of *Weli*,
and all the dwellers along *Namongeh*.
She wants to see *Kwai* dancing, summoning
Ngomba, he carries *Mozonje*, it drums for peace.
She wants to sit bare buttocks on the ground,
watch the matriarch as she cleanses her chest
with warm leaves from *Iroko* tree.

Let the rains come in June not August.

She can sing, *'Ewuwe, Emma ma we'*
with lines across her face
like wrinkles on the face of a battled-hardened soldier,
she wants to make airplanes
with mango leaves, placing
them in rivulets, to follow as
they go down the gutter,
into the stream, the river,
disappearing with her dreams,

Let the rains come in June not August,

August's rains are crueler.

In the distance, drummers play,
chiefs and their servants gather,
palm wine flowing, villagers dancing.

Children hide behind windows,
peeping for the face of *Nganya*,
(fierce juju) as if their time would come.
A boy and an old man sit across the field.
Wrestlers gather in *Ewoka ya Wezruwa*.
Women dress in fine garments.
Wrestlers jump up and down,
bare-chested, twisting their biceps.
Suitors will travel from far and wide,
the mating ritual has begun.

Let the rains come in June not August.

She wants to fish in *Mosreh*,
catching prawns with palm nuts as baits,
to roast and dine with banana leaves
to play hopscotch with *Enanga*
and learn to skip with no ropes.

When the rains come in June,
she will catch bullfrogs just below
the fountains of Woteke village,
buy ripe palm nuts in *Zroppo Zralli*,
sit under the Iroko tree gazing
at the mountains, counting the clouds
as they come and go.

Let the rains come in June not August.

She can hold hands with *Ikomi*,
like lovers do, play hide, and seek
between boulders abandoned
by the great volcano of eighty-six.
She can drift through tea plantations
when the rains come in June,
let the rains come in June, not August.
Truly, if Heaven is her father's land,
her father can keep it.

Bakweri: The '*Bakweri*' live on the slopes of Mount Hvako in South-western Cameroon, with a population of approximately 32,200 speakers. Their language, Bakweri, Baakpe (Guthrie 1953), or typically simply Mòkpè is classified as part of the Bantu family and is closely related to Bomboko, Isubu, Duala and other languages of the Duala group.

Evasrikuke: A type of bird that can be heard but is rarely seen. To hear it singing is a good luck omen.

Mbasri: Maize plant.

Ezruli: The smallest bird in the sunbird family.

Hvako: The *Bakweri* name for Mount Cameroon.

Weli: A place just below the Savannah, the fertile grounds of Mount Hvako.

Namongeh: A small stream, that feeds off waters from the mountain. The people on her banks rely on this water.

Kwai: A kite.

Ngomba: Porcupine, known for its mastery as a drummer.

Mozonje: A female drum, when played, it pleads for peace to reign in the land.

Iroko tree: It grows to almost 50 metres, 164 feet. It features a lot in Bakweri folktales and mythologies. It is feared and revered. It is on the side of the Iroko whilst watching the stick insect doing what looked like a ritual press-up that the millipede pleaded with the gods to render it blind and deaf. Thus, posing the rhetorical question: 'Can blindness be desired? What have those eyes seen to desire to see no more?' The Iroko tree is highly exploited for its timber.

'Ewuwe Emma ma weh': A song we would sing as children, it is infectious, it sends a signal. As one child starts singing, all the children in the neighbourhood would join in.

Mozre: A small stream that runs from the mountain through the village of Small Soppo, (Zroppo Zralli) all the way to the Atlantic Ocean, in Limbe, once called Victoria (1858-1982).

Nganya/Fierce juju: If you come face to face with this particular juju, you are cursed and develop an incurable disease.

Ewoka ya Wezruwa: Wrestling grounds.

Mosreh: A river.

Zroppo Zralli: The author's hometown in Cameroon. It is divided into three zones: Woteke, Wovilla and Wonganga. He is from Wovilla.

Forbidden

long
she
held
onto
an
apple
yours
knowing
it
would
poison
her
hungry
she
took
a
bite
after
all
you
predicted
her
fall.

Displacements

Bones

A distorted civilization,
is buried here.

Whorehouse of a duke, once
stood here.

In tight-fitting shoes, under
equatorial sun,
our grandparents waited here,

sweating.

In silence, they waited, singing
anthems to foreign kings
and their queens.

They were all here.

Can't you see the bones?

1982

In that year, we regressed to superstition,
turned to birds on treetops, buffeted by winds.
Our bird choirmasters turned with us, turned on us,
hissing. Then protesting birds, placards between beaks,
have wings removed, claws clipped.

There are new chiefs to chew on government bones
among them is *Ngarkah* a protestant bird,
rewriting his will, once titled *'Tears in Bantu House-Hold,'*
now, *'Forever choirmasters, We Smile.'*

Afterward there were years in prisons, fatalities,
elites with glittering *crowbow* heads
who sit at mahogany tables swallowing
Kentucky fried chicken, French beef stew,
Boulangerie, bones of famous *Ekulekule*,
who leave only scattered crumbs
for white-capped head chefs.

There is a new chief who brings us reincarnated
dead, brought forward as unsuspicious *Ekongi*.
Then vote-riggers, overdosing villagers
with chloroform, after thirty-eight years
he confesses *Ndondondume* is my name.

Crowbow: bald head in pidgin English.
Ekulekule: Tortoise, the wise one.
Ekongi: the dead, those belonging to the spirit world.
Ndondondume: a mythical beast of ill repute, a devil, a mythical beast, it lures people
into their doom, mishaps with its beautiful voice. Many people have left their marital
homes and entered into relationships with Ndondondume only to find out his true
nature when it was too late.

Love

In my voyage I see her
face, calling her many
names:
Namondo
Enjema
Emolana Eposi
Nyanngo'o
I write epistles to her:
Janu Jende o Liwor
Janu Kasri Kasri
Will she?
Won't she?
Who knows?
I carry
an old picture of her,
singing her many names.

Janu Jende o Liwor: Come let us go to the market. Once you start going
to the market together, it is a sign that the family approves your union.
Janu Kasri Kasri: Come quick, quick.

For Natalia

I was not destined to leave my bones on
the snow-filled terrains of Vladivostok.
This, I knew for sure, the treaty was already
signed between my maker and I,
although a stubbornness detained me.

I knew my maker would not leave me half-
way, in that lonely existence, swinging
through the doors of insanity, a continual
decent through hell, and her environs,
the snow-filled terrains of Vladivostok.

I hear it again in Old Russian Ballads,
that filled me with hope so I could not give up.
'Я вас любил: любовь еще, быть может' *
I loved you, this love can be again. It carried
my spirit home, when I was eating leftovers
from my mother's dirty pots. I have known love:
when we kissed, I felt your face in my hands.

I was not destined to leave my bones on
the snow-filled terrains of Vladivostok.
Memories are my hiding place, dreams
of hell and heaven intertwine, from here,
I saw the green fields of my distant home.

'Я вас любил: любовь еще, быть может'
I loved you, this love can be again.
* Alexander Pushkin

Great Grand Aunt Vera

There were no screams
no wailings no dancing,
nor choir groups singing,
just an empty bench, *the Lavuchka.*

Yesterday, Tetya
Vera was here.
Teaching me
"Kak Vam dela?"
Not *"Kak tebia dela, nor Kak
vas dela."* Intricacies in
Russian speak.

The *Lavuchka* speaks of time, knowing
when the children would come, and
when they would go.
Lavuchka is a resting place.

3:30, the pitter-patter of feet,
children, boys, girls, sitting,
gossiping, some crying.

'Mama ya khochu yedu?'
'Mother, can I please have food?'

At 5:30 pm
Lavuchka embraces teenagers, they
share one *'myasnoy pirog'* meat pie
between four.

At 7:00 pm
Lavuchka welcomes young adults playing
guitars, eating fried pumpkin seeds, *'semischki'*,
playing hide and seek behind shrubs and bushes,
dreaming of spring blossom.

At 8:30 pm
'Molodaya zhenshchina,' young
women come out in droves,

crying of failed careers,
'Ya khotel byt
balerinoy' talking of lost
love, then, just like they
came slowly, they
disappear.

Where are the men?

Lavuchka ignores men, they labour
in various *'Dachas'* fruit picking
sealing jars / jars of salted cucumber,
for when winter comes.

Valeria is always drunk.

At 9:30pm *Tetushka* Vera comes, sits on *Lavuchka*, she
speaks of the alignment of stars, of her three dead husbands,
the glory days of the Red Army, chasing Nazis across Siberia.
Her wrinkles like land markings, she speaks of permanent
longing, her neck moves slowly, scanning the horizon.

It has been three weeks now, children come
and go, young boys and girls, I saw them all
gossiping, playing guitar, eating *semischki*.
Three weeks, Tetushka Vera did not come out.

'Excuse me please, where is aunty Vera?'
извините, пожалуйста, где тетя Вера?

"She is gone."
"What do you mean, she is gone?"

"Three weeks ago, Tetya Vera died."

Velikaya babushka tetushka Vera
Great Grand Aunt Vera

I did not cry.
Tetya Vera died of age.

No wailings, no choir groups singing, just
a Russian bench which reminded me
every evening at 9:30 that Tetya Vera
was dead.

When They Came

Across the village gates, they
came, beyond the river
where two roads meet, they
came. Behind the wooden
house where we once played,
they came. Was it you?
Did you trim the hibiscus? They could
see us from beyond the hills.
Ndondondume, the beast, you left the
village gates open, you guided soldiers
onto her bed. They found her stiff at
dawn, mouth agape, lips blackened,
veins on her face popping, eyes
shouting, *"Ndondondume"*, the beast,
you left open the village gate, you
guided soldiers onto her bed.

Merci Pour Ton Coeur

On a junction, we stopped, resting our heads on stones, tired.

Side by side on
rustling leaves,
sleeveless, that
night we slept.

Desert sands separated us,
   speaking through winds
      blowing
                  that night they blew.

   Dreaming, building poets
gardens *mon ami, merci pour*
         ton Coeur

                           Abdel,
                           Abdel
                           Abdel

How many times must I whisper your name?
      Plagued, muscular-dystrophy-pained.

One by one I pray your
   poems turned to stars
                  eagles will fly them to your homeland.

                  Purifiers of language mocked.

El Sadat El Malaki flogged, publicly they
      planted cockroaches in your hair
                  stained the grave of your umbilical cord

                        Abdel

I shall paint cities
in poetry, a
vestry
                           for you at forty.

You are not an offender yet,
                    Upon your shoulders
                        a curse is placed.

                    Mon ami Abdel, merci pour ton Coeur.
In silence of night's walls
    of rooms crumbling,
        thoughts strangling,
    memories failing, I cry
        for you.

Must I stand in public, tear clothes
    on my back, declare myself insane
summon the thousand gods I detest?

Once upon a time we
        laughed.
Now, you do not remember my face, my name, I am a distant memory,
            lost, crowded out of your dying mind, slowly.

                        Intact
you left the Mullah's grumbling,
Swallows of Cymru greeted you,
                    a kiss on your cheek.

                    Daily,
    your crippling bones glued you to a
wheelchair. You die with every wind that
            blows. It blows.

                    Tonight, my pillow is wet.
            Abdel, *mon ami, merci pour ton Coeur.*

Mind

As my mind travels, ghost of Kuva keeps
me awake, his breath on my face drains
sleep, from my tired eyes, insomnia.

I see their faces on TV sets,
adrift in the blue Aegean Sea,

hares on snares, they scream, young
lives claimed by violent waves, chasing
dreams, finding a mirage, drowned.

Upon these shores I leave my footprints.

1986

Red Moon over lake Nyos,
doomsday whispers armed with drums,
survivors like ghosts of the apocalypse,
singing choruses of the end times.
Why have the gods forsaken us?

Red Moon over the poisonous lake,
salutations of umbra and penumbra.
Survivors like Old Testament eremite
from yonder, foretelling tales, turning
ghosts, consumed by gaseous light.

Red Moon, dogs in heat, barking.
One lone, dazed survivor. See her:
standing/stuttering/falling/holding
onto nearby railings. Did she invite
disaster by boiling beans overnight?

Red Moon over lake Nyos.
Noises, clamoring. They went to bed
and never woke up. The few, resurrected,
singing choruses of the end times.
Why have the gods forsaken us?

*Lake Nyos disaster, Bamenda, Cameroon, 1986: a limnic eruption on the 24th of August 1986 killed 1,746 people.

Memory

For Joyce Ashuntangtang

Just before dawn when the city bleeds,
the poet undresses in the dark and writes.
Witness, she pushes herself to tell
of prison cells and sharpened guillotines,
of how she sees thieves with cloaks and daggers,
their faces hanging on posters and billboards.

When the city bled, in the reddening dawn,
she saw the children, her children.
They were many and feeding on garbage
in bins and gutters, hungry as rats.
In their eyes, she saw before they did
the corpses they would be tomorrow.

A Witch

He wiped his sweat with two fingers and crossed the road to the graveyard. He saw epitaphs of various departed souls. He hummed love songs in darkness. Lost in thought, he met an old woman, a palm reader, holding a cat.

He remembered her words: "Behind this graveyard of fallen dreams a beautiful city awaits you. In that city, there are beds of roses, there are starlings in the skies just before dusk. Blackberries reach into the roads begging to be plucked from their stalks. There are blue and yellow lilies as far as eyes can see. On the roof of the house, where three paths cross, princess Farzana awaits you."

"Come closer," she said, for the witch was blind. "Go yonder my son, follow the path, at its gate shout 'Farzana', and the circle of this tragedy will end." He wiped his sweat with one finger. The witch handed him a letter. It said, "I will wait for the lights to go before I forget you. It is hard for you, even harder for me. There is nothing we can do but cry, peacefully." I will bow and listen to the music these winds bring. There's poison under my tongue, maybe, just maybe, I am only 24 hours away from you. Like the rain on his windowpane with its monotonous beats, she was gone.

When it Rains, I Think of You

Farzana,
and if you will return
alive or dead from that awful place,
the Al-Jawiywah prison,
meeting point for migrants and traffickers.
I think of you there,
where today, a quarrel brews:
to entertain themselves
the guards throw one toothbrush and paste
and watch inmates fight for it.
A mad woman paces up,
then down, an old man sits and stares.
Farzana is pregnant, skeletal,
she wants to leave this
makeshift jail where migrants
starve and soldiers
make merry over rum with traffickers.
When it rains I think of you,
Farzana,
and if you will return.

Inheritance (1998)

As the knives were placed on my skin
on that wintry night in Pechatniki, Moscow,
I did not feel pain.
I was happy to be killed by strangers.

I hated my father's family, those
who tricked me into exile.
All I could remember was the face
of my bleached-skin aunty *Eposi*,
who conspired with my sister
and my father's sister, to disinherit me.

So when I finally went back to Cameroon
and the village elders told me
that since her death, my Aunty *Eposi*
was unable to continue to the land of the spirit,
without my forgiveness, I thought

there is no harm for them, none,
going back to when the branch was first broken,
so easy for them: the here, the now.
But it is true what they say, *"The axe forgets
what the tree remembers."*

The core of my existence still touched,
shaken by her awful gaze, Aunty *Eposi*.
After nineteen years: her vile, wrinkled face,
rotten lips, dark gums, villainous tongue.

She was once my kin with whom I shared
leftover meals, now her bones are rejected,
ejected by her shallow grave. I promised
never to speak or write of her, 'till she withers
and winter's hard winds blow her skeleton
to pieces and her coffin spits her bones.

Cymru

Bus 18 to Ely

"You have a funny accent."

He said,
"You seem okay,"
he continued,

*"it is these half-castes, the Black people
born in this country, the ones spoiling
things for everyone."*

*"I saw Gary yesterday, selling legal highs
to kids in the alleyway."*

I have never met a black man called Gary,
I thought.

*"Do you know Gary's mum?
She's never had a job in her life, her children look like
those in the Red Cross leaflets, those children you see in Africa ....
Sometimes I wish Hitler won the war,
then we could keep this country clean...
so, where are you from, then, mate?"*

I paused.

Thoughts like pigeons flying in, then out of my head.
Yes, where was I from?
A Bantu tribesman.
A Bakweri boy.
How long must one stay in a place to become it?

"Funny enough, mate,
I am from Zimbabwe.
Do you know, all those white people who came to Zimbabwe with

Cecil Rhodes? Of the three million people Cecil killed, one million
survived.
Now, us, their great-grandchildren, have armed ourselves with poisoned
darts,
and crocodile's bile, killing Cecil Rhodes compatriots one by one."

"Blimey," he
said.
"How long have you been in this country?"

Again, I
paused.
Arrivals and departures mean different things to different migrants.

"Since yesterday," I
said.

As I reached into my bag, I asked him:
"Are you by any chance a white Zimbabwean?"

"Are you seriously hunting white Zimbabweans?" he
asked.

He pressed the stop button and
spoke to the driver, he brought
out his mobile phone.

"Excuse me, can I speak to the police?"

At my stop, just off
Grand Avenue, I said
"Thank you, drive."

"Excuse me, mate, are you really a white Zimbabwean head-hunter?"
the driver asked.

We laughed.

Dreams in Times of Corona

Door opened,
she spoke:
*"I have been pontificating
on the deteriorating situation in
Wovilla village."*

"Pardon?"
A beer can on the table, newspaper
clippings, magazines here, there.
Mwamballa meowing, idly.

Her garment was transparent.

*"So, tell me Mr…
can you play Ukulele?"*

Slowly, slowly,
I bulged, I painted
the brown of her eyes,
glowing, hibiscus–
shaped lips,
quivering eyelashes,
inviting, her dimples …
O, her dimples ….

I bring my face closer,
our lips meet.
We
we
we,
frightened,
I erase her,
leaving a dot.

Cymru

1

                                  Umbilical cord lost
uncertainties of exile, soles of her
    feet sore, her sojourn
treacherous, in silence of her
            dreams
    a stranger dies, an omen.

                                      In Abertawe
fingers point in direction of her birth, her tongue
                    cut
    she carries her head in a bowl, sharp blade dig
                            harvesting her memory.

In the uncertainties of exile,
            she once
                danced like a jester.

2

She dresses like a sweet-scented GARDEN:
her smile polite, her speech like morning dew
kissing mother earth, drip by drip, aroma of fresh
cut grass, autumn leaves in dark yellow and grey.
She is no longer blind, head bowed to earth touching
grasshoppers and gregarious ants who shout of her beauty.
For many years you resided inside her as a memory,
not a tightrope, but a fountain. She followed your smiles
in reveries every time she saw you, she anticipates
your departure with sorrow.

3

            Wry smile, her garment clear
                as light reaching a

closed eye. That is how she greeted me. Must I
define her? In her, I remember childhood, in her
embrace, I knew all would not be lost. A wry smile,
her garment clear as light, that is how she greeted me.

For Namondo, My Wife

When she laughs, you see her
Mbanyanya, a dance between
upper and lower lips.
My quest for her starts here.
On the morning we met
Namondo wore a black dress
that flowed to her knees ...
Jejayeeeeeeeee Namondo
Munyangor Amaja ...

When we said farewell,
Namondo cried,
she carried a basket of *Ndah*
from the market
to my mother's kitchen, her
black dress stained with sweat
and water from coco yams.

When I return,
we shall sit round the fire
I will sing to Namondo,
a bird song. I will carry her
a flowery blossom,
in memory of the moment
we met.
Munyangor Amaja.

Mbanyanya: A diastema, the gap in the front teeth. It is seen as a thing of beauty.
Munyangor Amaja: 'Your husband has come, your husband is here'.

Homeland

We cry for you,
here in our diaspora,
your children wandering barefoot,
are treated like knaves
with no names,
chasing goldstones,
silver slates,
grandfather sold for broken mirrors.
Where are our heroes?
Your tears taste of rape.
We cry for you,
"A child given Sellotape to fix their broken biscuits".*
Did we not undress on the banks of the river for you?
These are not pictures of us:
bloated belly, *kwashiorkor*, our wrinkled shinbones gained
sitting by the fire when the rains came.
Mothers of the mountains,
fathers of the seas,
why must your children walk on dried leaves?
Mokele mbembe, river deity, the one who roams Congo Basin,
why are our dreams lost?
Are they waiting for us in the lands beyond the horizons?
Will you open the floodgates after one thousand years?
Mokele mbembe, river deity, you alone know
where our dreams have gone,
why we wander.

*'A child given Sellotape …' from Ifor ap Glyn, the National Poet of Wales.
Kwashiorkor. A severe form of malnutrition.

South

In houses like broken mirrors,
we are shattered. On Sundays
we sing of love and through lightning,
we see the faces of poets, our dearest
departed. Those who had ears, talked
of the president, a dictator croaking
like a dying frog just before dusk.

Today the clouds of Cymru are heavy.
In Cameroon there were no watering holes
in the summer. And those poets who crossed
the river Mungo were pregnant.
Coming South, they gave birth to:
crocodiles, snakes, alligators, centipedes
scorpions, and us.

Smoke on the horizon, a new South rising
holding bush lamps, we stood still,
and we saw dead poets, sage
Mbella Sone
Dipoko,

"All the debates, resolutions, minutes, and decisions in poems
we shall assemble regardless of race ...."
Speak, Mola, speak.
"Let us all be poets." ★

We saw late Bate Besong,
drifting in ecstasy, floating in his
thoughts. Peace sir, peace.

We saw Mola Ndoko,
He spoke of
"Meyanna meeh Mopkwe"
"Ngowa aveli ndi Ngowa"

These men are Gods.
We saw skeletons of our grandmothers before
they joined spirits in the forest beyond.
Dearest departed poets in the village behind
the great *Meyolis* of South, our mothers cry,
their tears for us.

*Line from 'The Tenderness Manifesto', a poem by late Mbella Sonne Dipoko
Mbella Sonne Dipoko: 1936-2009. A poet, novelist, and painter. One of the foremost
contributors of Literature in English in Cameroon. I never met the great man, while he
was alive. I have met him several times reading his poems.
Bate Besong: 1954-2007. He stands tall amongst Cameroonians on the South of the River
Mungo as a giant of literature. His legacy looms large, we sing praises to him, a voice of
decency. For two hours, in 1995, I was honoured to be in his presence. He sat in our class
in Upper sixth Molyko, Buea for two hours without saying a single word.
Mola Ndoko: d.2012. He was a role model *par excellence*. He is one of the greatest Bakweri
icons, a fountain of knowledge. As children, we would wake up very early in the morning
just to listen to him talk on the radio.

Meyanna meeh Mopkwe: Bakweri proverbs.
Ngowa aveli ndi Ngowa: 'A pig will remain a pig'.
Meyolis: Hills.

Brothers

Our friendship
dances in colours:
Zroppo Zralli
Likoko Membeya
we followed the whispering of sunbirds to
Ewoka ya Wezruwa.
That day, we danced
in absence of fortune tellers,
fires of yearning,
burning.
What did the music say, *Mola*?
What did it say? We
became elephants running
down *Savannah Mbetetus*
lusting, *Molikilikili,*
pushing down then up, we
left before sunset
'Jejayeeeeeeeee'
in the distance,
on its balcony *Kwai* dances
calling for the rains to come.

Likoko Membeya: A small village where we attended secondary school
Mola: uncle, elder. It is rude to call people by their first names especially when
they are older than you, hence *mola*.
Mbetetus: fireflies.
Molikilikili: the Stick insect, extremely resilient in Bakweri and Bantu mythology.
You would come across the Molikilikili on the bark of huge trees, performing what
looks like a ritual press-up. If questioned, it would answer by telling you it is trying
to push the tree until it falls to the ground.
Kwai: kite.

The Grey Book

My mind wonders what treasures are hidden within your spine. Behind these fine lines should I pick you up and peruse? My eyes see an emerald island with sea breezes. My heart beating faster with every page turned, I wonder what lies ahead. The shyness of her smile bewitches me, an umbrella-like shadow it casts upon my soul. And no, I did not dream of her, my heroine. I watched her coming in fast-forward through these pages, *'La Belle Dame Sans-Merci'*, my eyes trembling every time she appeared. The melody of her voice. With her on horseback, we rode along a beach through coral stalagmites, picking shells in tidepools. We danced along the shorelines of a small province, using mangrove trees for firewood, cooking red crabs. They too were in season. Euphoria, through these pages, I see you, charmed by your unearthly songs. Through the pages of this grey book we dance together, towards that shore. I wait, reading between the lines, slowly.

When Children Cry

She sits on the bus: grey tracksuit,
Nike trainers, battered. Her pram
rickety, like an old wheelbarrow,
baby's face painted with mucus.

Mucus, I hope.

Baby cries, his feeding bottle inviting him.

Half a spliff on her left ear, the smell, possessing the bus,

driving into

St. Mellon's with a red lighter in her left hand,

fingernails like a low-paid fruit picker,

open can of Boost,

sure, the baby has one too.

Baby
cries.   *I am going to kill you just wait, let me*
get to St. Mellon's

I have to go and see my solicitors

job centre has only gone and stopped my payment

Universal credit is a b....... d I tells you,
I was only late for five minutes.
The ring chaining her lips to her nose fell,

she cried.

Flashback/Shakespeare

Lear, in the grounds of Trinity Church ....

Consanguineous events trailing,
                pendulum swinging, leaves
                                falling,
spells, revealing flashbacks,
                            dark, constant Déjà vu,
                    butterfly thinking itself a bird,
                                    it can't be so ....

I am Odewale current,
king of Kutuje, fathered
Ojowola, wife of late
king Adetusa.

Soothsayer Babatunde proclaims ails of your
                        kingdom lay in your father's hands, curse of
                                    Gods complete.

*A third, more opulent than your sisters, speak. Nothing can come out of nothing.
'Father, as happy as I am, I cannot heave my words into my mouth, I love your
majesty according to my bonds, no more no less.' 'Mend your speech young lady,
else it mars your fortunes.' 'Father, you have begot me you have loved you have
bred me. I cannot marry like my sisters and love my father all.'*

There, over there, beyond hills and faraway,
                        Edmund is grinning, a puppet on the strings of
Goneril and Regan. And I raged against
                    the destroyers of my father's grave.

      Turbulence mimics my heart's storms, eruptions.

                        Blow winds and crack your cheeks! Rage! Blow!
I took solace in a
place, a cold
infested room
with men,
women,

old,
grey hairs, faces rock solid:
Nebuchadnezzar, Moscow.

My father was not old,
not broken by age,
should not have been the first fruit to fall.

Forked their tongues,
Duchess of Cornwall, Duchess of Albany!
Treachery in high places.

The whip fell on my back, how my back hurts.

Those who lived under phosphorus clouds,
fenced themselves, departed souls roamed,
questions asked, *'where is the King, my master?'*

Today, my clan, house of Kange, house of Lyonga,
strangled webs weaved ...
Land of our mothers.
Rotimi Ola drunk on palm wine juice.

Lear in the grounds of Trinity church.

My father rests in in his ancestral
shrine, I speak.

Zugunruhe

Silence, as morning sun
uncovers her beauty,
trees swaying from side to side,
her black feathers glitter.
She smiles despite wounds
on her left ankle. She is
moving slowly, squinting
as if recalling a distant memory …
Other birds dance round an old Cedar tree,
some play hide and seek with leaves,
their eyes wandering the distant slopes
of their temporary homes.
Flexing plumes as if with an *Au revoir,*
a goldfinch stretches, a seasoned boxer.
Preparing for battle against the tides,
it digs for seeds, a last supper.
Some gather by the fireside,
clinging on the wings of fireflies,
flashing their buttocks as guides.
A mountain goat chews on its cud, dreamily.
Small black bird jumps up and down on one spot.
Invocations:
swallows like cold war spies
peeping through rock cracks
waiting for departure.

Zugunruhe: The experience of migratory restlessness: I came across this behaviour
whilst reading Ruth Padel's book *We Are All From Somewhere Else.* When it is time
to migrate, birds in cages would demonstrate *zugunruhe*.

Acknowledgements

Acknowledgements are due the magazines, books and websites where some of these poems first appeared: 'When They Came' was first published as 'Ndondondume' in *The 3 Molas* (Carreg Gwach,2020). Thanks to the other 2 Molas: Ifor ap Glyn and Mike Jenkins.

Some of these poems have also been featured on BBC Wales and BBC Radio 4, thanks to the producers of these programmes. 'If Heaven Is Her Father's Land …' and 'Bones' have been published in the *Wild Court* poetry journal, published by the English department of King's College London. 'South' quotes a line from 'The Tenderness Manifesto', a poem by the late Mbella Sonne Dipoko.

Diolch yn fawr to Llandeilo Festival, Cardiff Books Festival, Canton Book Festival. Special thanks to Peggy Hughes, Ellie Reeves, and Florence Reynolds at International Literature Showcase, National Centre for writing Norwich and The British Council England and British Council Netherlands. Also diolch to Wales Arts International and to Literature Wales for your continued support and belief. Further thanks to Erian James and Palas Print Bookshop in Caernarfon.

Many thanks too, to the generous writing community at Swansea University: Professor Kellerman and the poets and authors: Menna Elfyn, Dai George, Dr Francesca Rhydderch, Owen Sheers, and Elaine Canning. Thanks are due very much to the Swansea University MA groups for Poetry 1 and Poetry 2, 2019-2020 whose feedback and critique helped shape this collection. Also thanks to the writing students and staff at Dylan Thomas Centre in Swansea.

Thanks are due to: The Hay Festival Writers at Work and the Scribbler Tour team: Aine Venables, Jenny Valentine, Paul Elkington, and Daniel Morden. To Newport and Gwent Literary Club. To Cathy Brown, *Seamus Heaney: HomePlace Bellaghy*, for your wonderful reception during the Jaipur Literature Festival.

Thank you to Professor Ruth Padel for her helpful feedback and her inspirational book *We Are All From Somewhere Else* (Penguin, 2020). Thanks are also due to the staff at Aberystwyth University. Thanks as well to poets

Sudeep Sen and Jackie Kay, author Jon Gower, to Lyndy Cooke, editor Amy Wack and to Seren for bringing this work into the public domain.

Thanks to Amara Chimeka and Purple Shelves my publishers in Lagos, Nigeria. Thanks for taking my writing back to the continent where it all started. Further thanks to African Writers Trust in Uganda, The African Festival for Emerging Writers, Cameroon. Thanks also to: H.E. Churchill Ewumbue, Mola Dibussi Tande, Iya Florence Ayissi, Professor Humphrey Ndi and to Professor Joyce Ashuntangtang. Merci Nnane Ntube, mon ami Raoul Djimeli et Divine Mbutoh, our wrestling match is still pending.

Thank you as well, Jolie Iya Efeti, my daughter, for her patience with my early drafts.

Notes on Cameroon

The Republic of Cameroon is sometimes referred to as 'Africa in miniature' for its geological, linguistic, and cultural diversity. On the Gulf of Guinea in west-central Africa, it is home to 25 million people. After World War I, its territories were split between England and France. Its natural features include beaches, deserts, mountains, rainforests, and savannas. Its highest peak is Mount Cameroon (Hvako or Fako) in the southwest. Its cities with the largest populations are Douala on the Wouri River, its economic capital and main seaport, and Yaoundé, its political capital. Cameroon is well known for its native music styles, particularly Makossa and Bikutsii, and for its successful national football team.

Notes on Cymru: Wales

Wales is a country in southwest Britain, known for its dramatic mountain landscapes and for over 1600 miles of coastline, including Pembrokeshire and Snowdonia National Parks. Its native language is Welsh, one of Europe's oldest literary languages and still spoken by almost 900,000 of its roughly three million population. Established under the Government of Wales Act in 1998, the Senedd (The Welsh Parliament) is in Cardiff is responsible for a range of devolved policy matters. Wales is also called 'Land of Song' for its rich choral traditions. Rugby is the popular national game.

From the author: notes on Bakweri

My ancestors know me by the name Ngalle meaning a creator of thunder. Eric Charles only came to be my name when I was 'baptised'. On the day of my baptism, I lost my name and more importantly, I lost my prized chicken. As a thank you for baptising me, my mother donated my chicken to the missionaries. I am from Buea, the onetime capital of German Kamerun 1884-1916 (I am not proud of this fact).

From when I could speak, I was taught Bakweri, my mother tongue. In school we were beaten until we submitted to the fact that we were only allowed to speak French and English. To rebel against this new imposed tongue, we developed pidgin English, a language spoken by Nigerians, Cameroonians, Liberians, and people from Sierra Leone. Cameroon stands divided today along old colonial lines, between the English and the French spheres of influence. The average Cameroonian speaks at least four languages.